# Find Your Inner Truth

### Written by

## Yinuo Tian

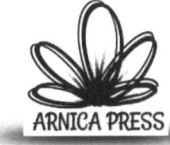
ARNICA PRESS

Published by ARNICA PRESS

www.ArnicaPress.com

Copyright © 2019 Yinuo Tian

Cover Art by Yinuo Tian

All rights reserved.

Art by Yinuo Tian

Written by Yinuo Tian

All rights reserved. No part of this publication may be reproduced or transmitted in any form or by any means, electronic or mechanical, including all digital form of media without prior written permission from the Author and publisher

Author Website:

www.yogabijaa.com

ISBN: 978-1-7336446-2-4

The material contained in this book has been written for informational purposes and is not intended as a substitute for medical advice, nor is it intended to diagnose, treat, cure, or prevent disease. If you have a medical issue or illness, consult a qualified physician.

# Find Your Inner Truth

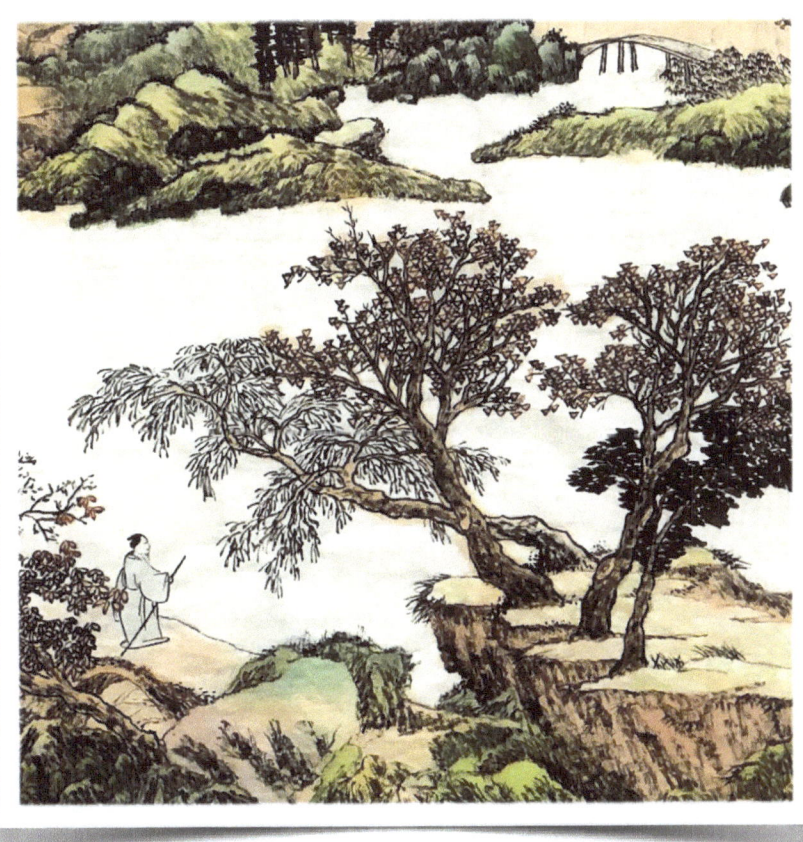

富足 智慧 幸福 創造

謙遜 勇氣 跨越 豐盛

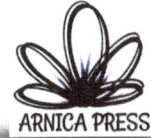

ARNICA PRESS

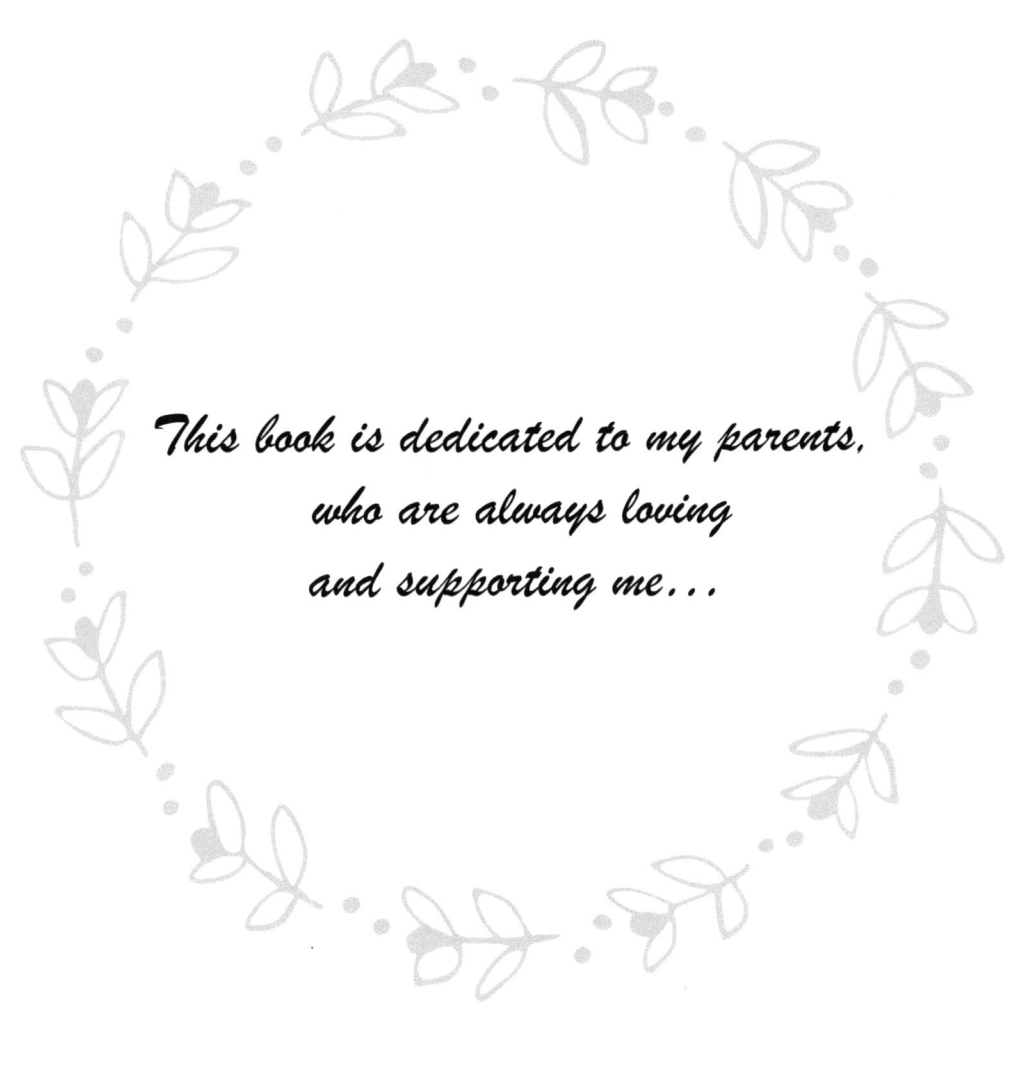

*This book is dedicated to my parents,
who are always loving
and supporting me…*

# Table of Contents

Introduction ..................................................................................... 9

Humility ........................................................................................ 10

Courage ........................................................................................ 14

Rebirth .......................................................................................... 18

Creation ........................................................................................ 22

Growth .......................................................................................... 26

Maturity ........................................................................................ 30

Wisdom ......................................................................................... 34

Self~reflection ............................................................................... 38

Blessings in Disguise .................................................................... 42

Overcoming Obstacles .................................................................. 46

Letting Go ..................................................................................... 50

Prosperity ...................................................................................... 54

Happiness ..................................................................................... 58

Abundance .................................................................................... 62

Journey of the Soul ....................................................................... 66

Acknowledgments ........................................................................ 71

About the Author .......................................................................... 73

*Find Your Inner Truth ~ YINUO TIAN ~ 8*

# *Introduction*

As a child growing up in China, I never really thought about what to do later in life. I only knew that in order to have a bright future, I must study hard and get into a good university. My hard work at school was well paid off when I was fortunate to receive a full scholarship from Singapore at the early age of 16. Following a popular trend at that time, I chose Electrical and Computer Engineering as my major, and furthered my studies in pursuing a Master's Degree in Applied Finance. After successfully graduating and receiving my Master's, I entered the finance industry with full force and was working intensely for three years.

Surrounded by perpetual high stress, and constant preoccupation of the main player of that industry – money, I quickly realized, it was not the life I wanted to live. One morning I woke up, made my decision, and resigned.

At that time, I had already been practicing yoga for more than seven years, but I was not sure if yoga should be the path into my future. However, somehow the Universe pushed me into more serious and in-depth yoga studies, and led me to an eye-opening deep spiritual journey.

It has not been an easy odyssey. After bumping my head here and there while walking on this extraordinary path, I finally managed to connect with my heart, my true self, and clearly find my passion and direction.

It was also during this self-discovery journey that I realized I had another gift. I could paint. For me, painting is a form of meditation, a profound spiritual practice. Although I consider myself just a beginner in Chinese painting and my paintings may have many flaws in the professional artists' eyes, to me, they are still my greatest treasures. I express my creativity and spiritual knowledge through the stroke of the brush, and put my heart into each piece I create.

Every painting presented in this book conveys a spiritual message. It is my wish to share these messages with all Souls who are searching for their true selves. With deep affection from my heart, I hope you find this book helpful and inspiring.

With humility in service,

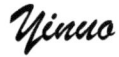

# *Humility*

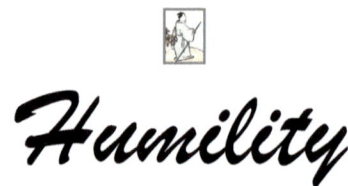

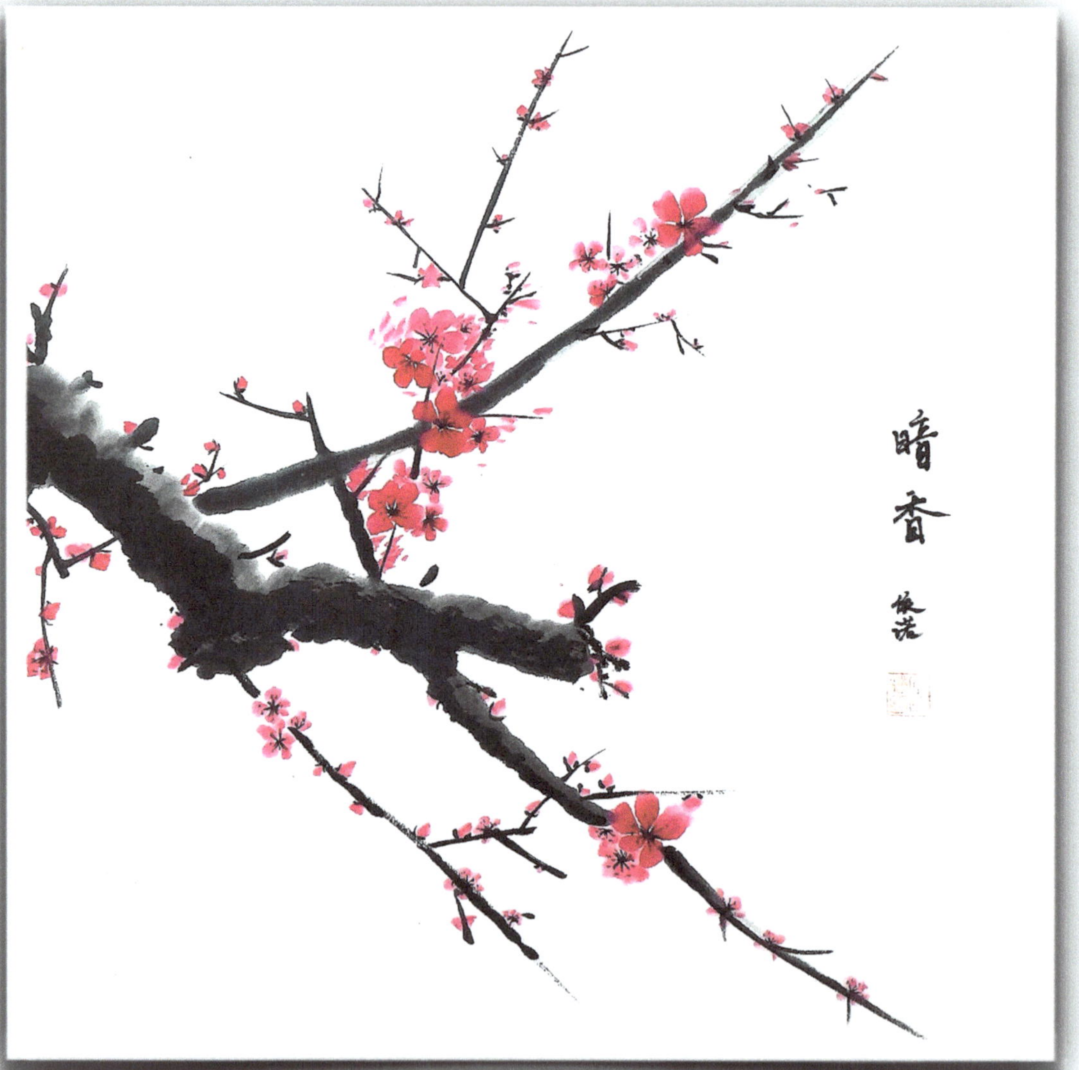

Find Your Inner Truth ~ YINUO TIAN ~ 10

*"Only humility knows how to appreciate and admire the good qualities of others."*

*~ Sri Chinmoy ~*

The plum blossom flower comes in different colors, yet never with an overpowering fragrance. It always blooms in the freezing winter, when all other flowers fade. In Chinese culture, the plum blossom is described as one of the "four gentlemen"[1] and it symbolizes the character of humility.

In today's self-centered world, humility has become a seriously lacking characteristic; and what is even worse, is that we are not even aware of this lack. With various social media tools, we are too used to be in the spotlight, craving for others' recognition and respect. Oftentimes, we talk about our life, our achievements and problems, but do not spend time listening to other people's talk, even when they are a part of our immediate family or within the circle of close friends. We are always busy "being ourselves", so it becomes a norm to judge others according to our own perspectives.

Humility is about caring about others' well-being ahead of thinking solely about ourselves. When we are humble, we are able to put ourselves into other people's shoes, and we start to experience a profound sense of resonance with others. We understand that we are all in the same boat, we are all one. We breathe the same air, we drink the same water. We all have good times and face challenges in life. Knowing this, we are willing to listen more instead of just talk about ourselves, and it becomes natural to open the heart, be more accepting, loving and giving. We begin to learn and support each other in many different ways in life.

When we are humble, we are also able to listen to our inner voice. Other people's views towards us are no longer as important, because we know who we truly are. Humility is not about denying our strength, but acknowledging our weakness. We will not be bothered whether people honor us or not. We are who we are. In this way, we are able to demonstrate sincere honesty and great compassion, towards ourselves, as well as others.

Humility is the longing to serve. With the gentleness of the heart, we respect others' opinions, value our interactions, and become more understanding. Compassionately, we are willing to love and serve the society as a whole.

What can we do in order to prevent going in the opposite direction of humility, which is described as arrogance, pride, self-centeredness? One of the techniques I find very useful is to maintain a thankful heart. Early in the morning, during the day, or before I go to the sleep at night, I like to think of the blessings I have received every now and then. I am always surprised at how effective this technique is in diminishing my pride.

*1.The "Four Gentlemen" refer to plum blossom, orchid, bamboo and chrysanthemum.*

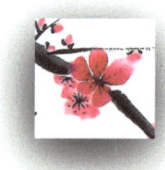

## *Suggestions*

At least once a day, make it a habit to express gratitude in front of a mirror.
Look into your own eyes and speak out loud your gratitude.
Your words can express anything that you feel thankful of at that moment.
Repeat this exercise at least once a day, or as many times as you wish.

## *Inner Search*

Am I practicing humility in life?
What can I do to live with more humility?
How should I cultivate humility with my family and in workplace?

## *Affirmation*

**I am completely humble and willing to love and serve more.**

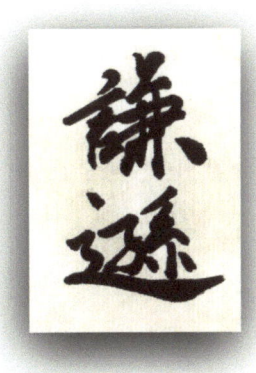

# *Courage*

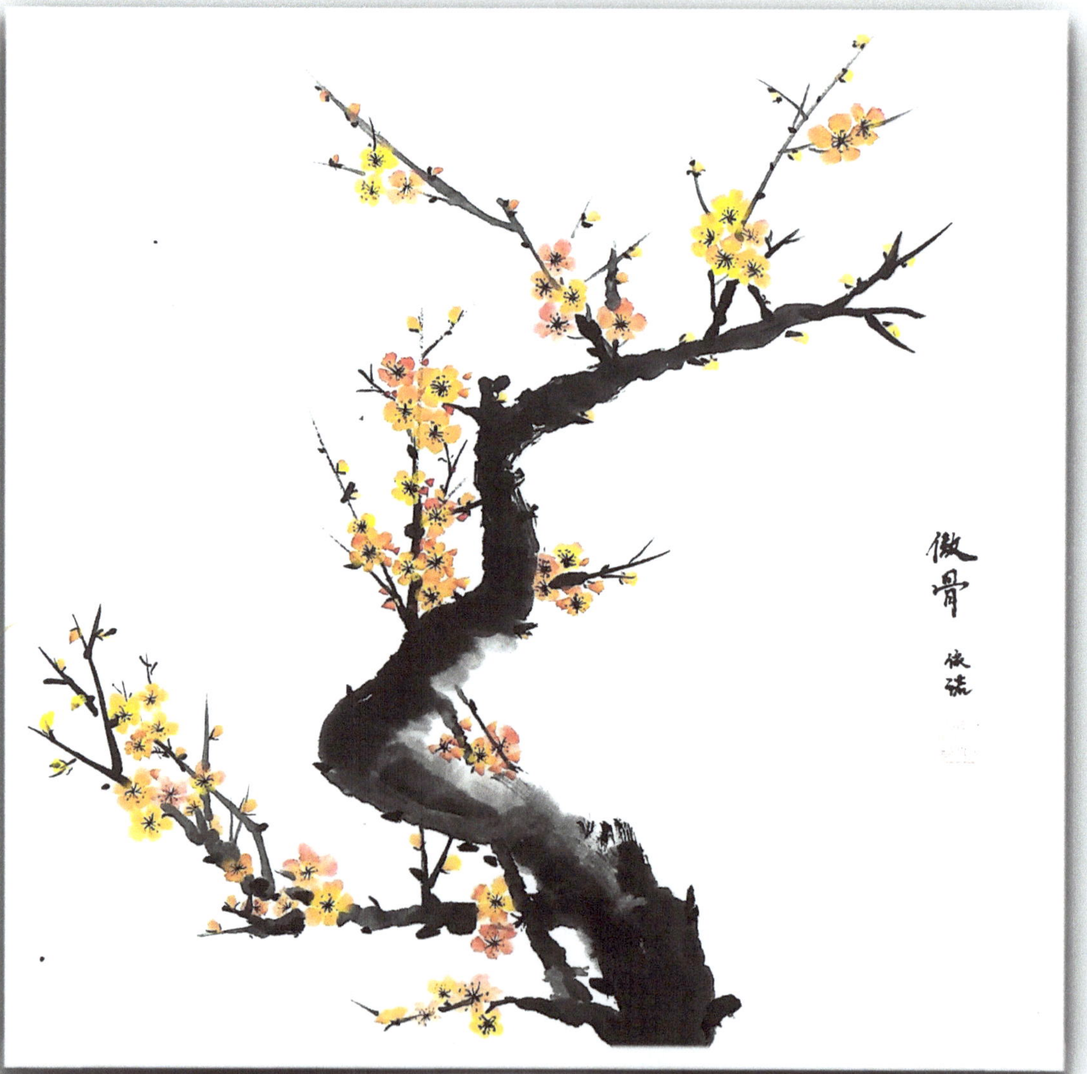

Find Your Inner Truth ~ YINUO TIAN ~ *14*

*"It takes courage to show up and become who you really are."*

*~ E. E. Cummings ~*

We all experience fears and anxieties when facing certain challenges in life. What is your reaction when you find yourself in a difficult situation? Do you shy away and hide as if nothing has happened? Do you create all kinds of excuses in order not to deal with it directly and immediately? Or do you choose to take actions with bravery, admit to yourself and declare to the world wholeheartedly that "I am ready", although deep inside you know you are still afraid?

Courage is the ability to overcome fear, face the difficulties in life, and do things that need to be done despite the fact that we are afraid to do them. No matter what happens, a courageous person always chooses to go out there with passion and take necessary steps towards their goals, never letting fear stop them.

Being courageous is not easy. Going through the path of courage, we have to step out of our comfort zone. There are always risks involved. For example, you probably are earning a decent income and living comfortably with your 9-to-5 job, however, deep inside you always hear the tiny little voice telling you to resign from your current job and travel the world. We all could come out with a whole list of risks involved here, what if this happens, what if that happens, so on and so forth. Are you ready to take such risks? Are you ready to follow what your heart and intuition tells you to do?

Being courageous could also mean to go against the norm, how ready are we for that? Do we acknowledge the differences between ourselves and other people? Are we embracing such differences? We all know who we really are and what we truly want to become, however, many times we choose to let others convince us to be someone else. It is important to draw healthy boundaries in life, truly believe and speak up for yourself.

Without courage, life does not terminate, but it certainly shrinks and fades away as time goes by. To cultivate courage in life, first and foremost, we must be totally honest with ourselves. Learn to accept ourselves completely, acknowledge our strengths and weaknesses. Once we are comfortable with our true self, we are able to show the whole world our true colors, and shine with confidence.

Now it is the time to step out with courage, follow the heart, embrace new beginnings, new people, and new energies.

## Suggestions

Take out your journal and list down your strengths and weaknesses.
Take your time, do not rush, be ready to take days, weeks or even months to complete the list. While doing this, acknowledge everything on the list without any judgment.
Once you are completely comfortable with the whole list,
look at the items that you want to improve,
make a plan on how to take actions.

## Inner Search

Do I feel courageous?
How could I be more courageous?
What daily courageous action can I add to my life?

## Affirmation

**I am full of courage and I stand up for myself.**

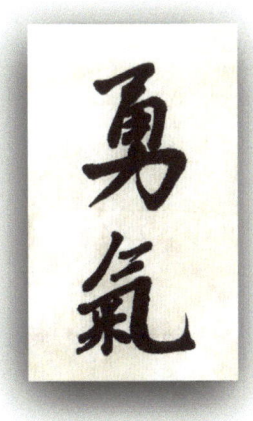

# Rebirth

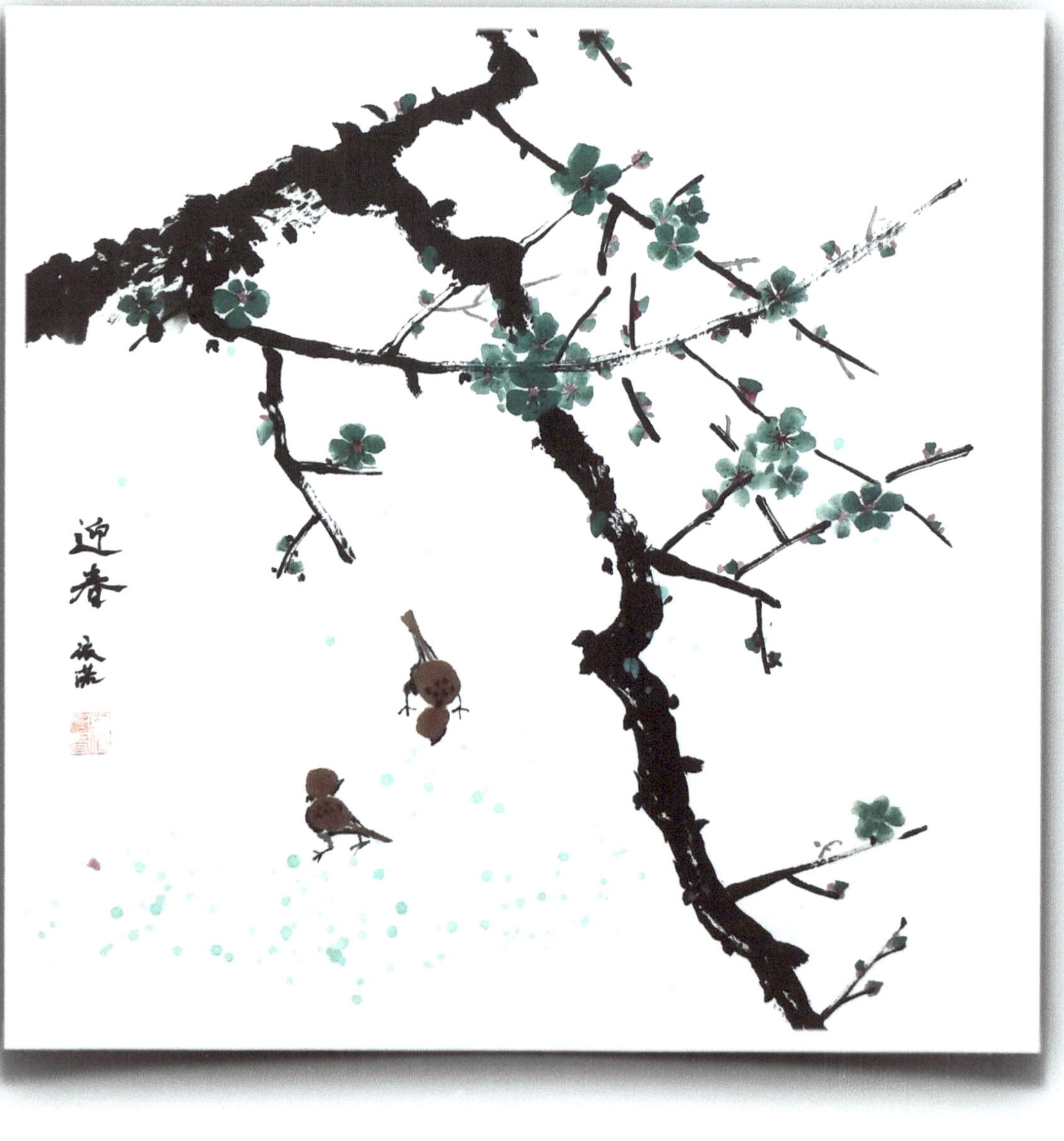

Find Your Inner Truth ~ YINUO TIAN ~ *18*

*"Our greatest glory is not in never falling, but in rising every time we fall."*

*~ Oliver Goldsmith ~*

Life is like a book, we live through different experiences in different chapters, and we keep closing the old chapters and opening new ones as time goes by. Rebirth takes place whenever we reach the end of the previous chapter and decide to open a new one. An end always brings a new beginning. The past is over, no matter what was experienced and how we feel about it. We all receive the choice to experience a brand new chapter in life.

I am pretty sure that all of us have such "rebirth" feelings when we complete a project, relocate to a new place, make new friends, or have a major shift in life. The feeling of rebirth is also experienced when we shed our old habits and energies that no longer serve us, like a snake sheds its skin. Whenever this happens, we learn to look at things and life from a totally different and new perspective. We are willing to open the heart to embrace the newer and lighter energy, feeling totally excited to start something different, in a brand new and hopeful way.

If we dig deeper, it is not difficult to understand that rebirth only happens when one is ready. A successful life transformation is for the brave ones. If we are not ready for the shift, we would not experience a revitalizing and refreshing rebirth. Furthermore, this life transformation does not happen out of the blue, there is a ton of preparation work involved. From the moment the decision is made, to the time when the actual shift occurs, every minute matters, every second counts.

I love observing babies and toddlers. They are full of curiosity and passion. Whenever they open their eyes, they begin their exploration of new things and new adventures. To them, each exploration is like a rebirth, through which they get revitalized and refreshed. I cannot help asking myself, since when, have we adults, lost interest in such explorations? And since when, have we allowed rebirth only after major life events? Look at the babies, their life changes daily due to their new explorations which lead to their frequent rebirth. Similarly, once we allow rebirth to happen more frequently, once our attitude and perception change, our world can also become completely different from a few months, a few weeks or even a few days ago. Isn't that be exciting?

Accepting your own rebirth is a courageous decision. It brings unexpected gifts for sure. Are you brave enough to make such a decision on a daily basis? There is a famous Chinese saying, "A journey of a thousand miles begins with a single step." Let us not wait for a better starting point, for every moment is the perfect starting point.

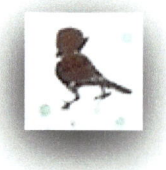

### *Suggestions*

Every night before bedtime, reflect on what happened during the day.
Ask yourself this question: what can I do to make tomorrow a better day?
The answer can be part of the intention setting for your next beautiful day.

### *Inner Search*

Am I allowing rebirth to occur?
Am I capable of and open to my own rebirth?
What is the new version of me that I expect after rebirth?

### *Affirmation*

**I welcome changes into my life and I enjoy the experiences of rebirth, revival and rejuvenation.**

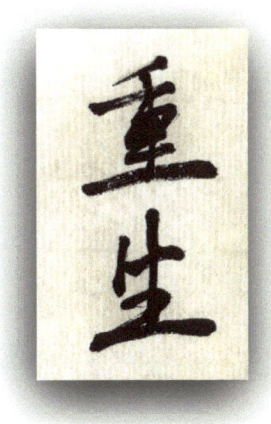

# *Creation*

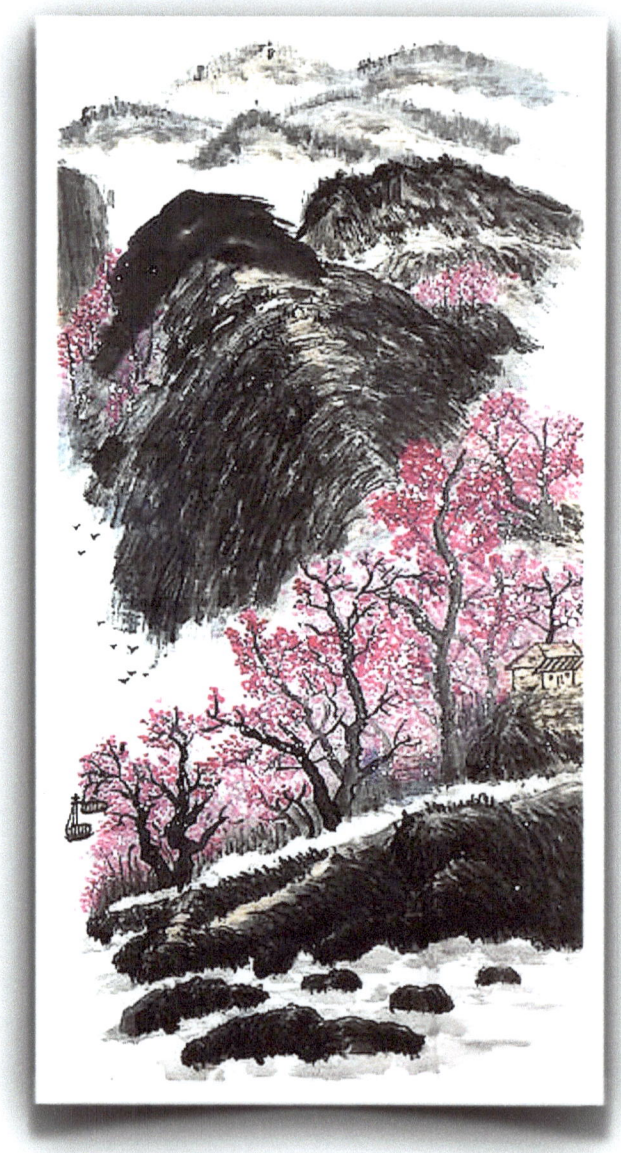

Find Your Inner Truth ~ YINUO TIAN ~ *22*

*"Create the highest, grandest vision possible for your life, because you become what you believe."*

*~ Oprah Winfrey ~*

Have you ever set a weight loss goal, but failed to follow a healthy diet or lifestyle?
In the end, the ideal weight was never achieved.
Have you ever wasted time, energy, and money on something that you were not really interested in, and as a result, you gave up your life's dream which could have brought great satisfaction and happiness?

I am sure above examples sound very familiar. Whenever such things happen, many of us start blaming others, complaining about the current state, pointing fingers at people and circumstances. We convince ourselves those caused these results.

Our life is an outcome of the choices we make. However, we have been trained to accept the life that other people impose on us since our youth. Many of us are living a mundane life, and we become numbed about the choices at hand. We pray for better things to happen in our life; we allow other people to decide where we are going. As a result, we are never happy or we find ourselves in the middle of nowhere.

It is very important to understand that we are creative human beings, we are more powerful than we think, and we have the ability to create the life we really want. How can we accomplish that?

First of all, take back your responsibility . No one can help us create the life we want, except ourselves. We are totally in charge of our destiny. If there is something that we do not like about our current life, it is time to start making better choices. It may not be necessary to make huge shifts, sometimes small changes can quickly make our life today a little better than yesterday.

Clarity is also an important aspect in creation. Follow the heart, know clearly where you are heading to. Deep in the heart, we all have a sense of what type of life we want to live, however, the mind is always tricking us, by making external factors look more important. Learn to separate the heart desire from mind games.

The next step is taking action. Once we set a goal, we need to evaluate and measure our actions towards that goal. What are the necessary steps we need to take? It is ok to take baby steps, as long as we are getting closer to the goal. Be patient. Believe that it will happen.

Remember, our life is a creation of our own thoughts and actions. Create a life which feels good inside, not a life that only looks good from the outside. The universe always responds to our requests. Sit back and watch the magic unfold. Creation is fun.

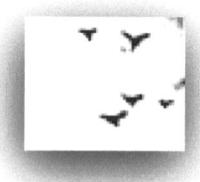

## *Suggestions*

Be mindful of your life events, no matter how small or big. Reflect how these events are created by your own thoughts, words, actions and reactions. Keep this in a journal.

## *Inner Search*

Do I recognize I play a decisive role in creating my life?
Am I allowing and expressing my creativity?
Do I have a desire to develop my creativity?

## *Affirmation*

**I create my own reality and I take full responsibility for my own life.**

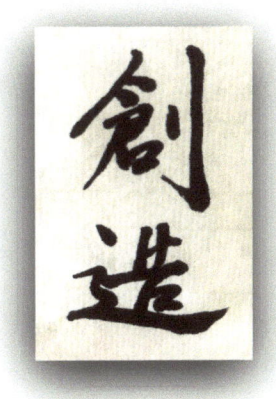

# *Growth*

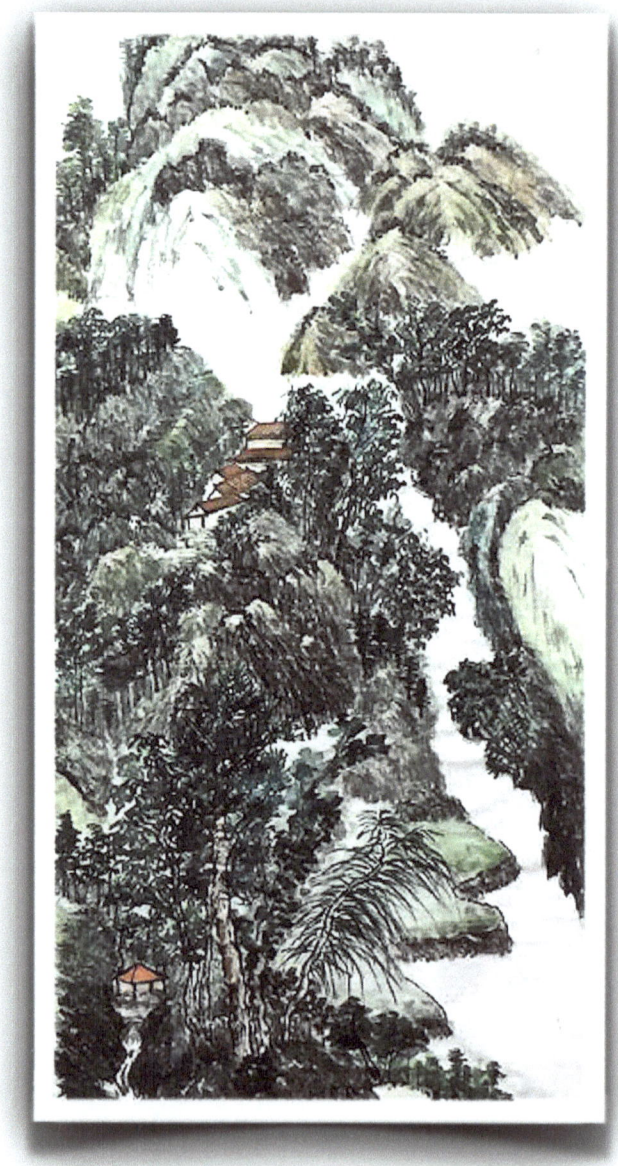

Find Your Inner Truth ~ YINUO TIAN ~ *26*

*"I am always doing that which I cannot do, in order that I may learn how to do it."*

*~Pablo Picasso~*

You may have heard about the medical term "growing pains". It generally happens to kids aged between 3 and 12 years, who are growing up very fast. The pain is usually in the legs and knees. There is no treatment for such pain, therefore the kids have to endure it till it naturally goes away.

We all experience pain in our lives. Looking through the tough periods of my life, I realize that with growth there comes always also pain, sufferings and discomfort. I learn valuable lessons through those periods.

When we are down, it is hard for us to see the way out. We may feel such great pain and disappointment, that the recovery seems far away. However, we have the power to make a conscious choice about what to gain with this growing pain. Do we want to take the opportunity and grow, or do we want to give up and allow the pain to consume us?

Growth and comfort are rarely friends. In order to grow, we need to welcome the pain and discomfort. It takes courage to accept the pain as "a guest in your house". Successful people normally have a growth-oriented mindset, they always welcome the pain, and tolerate it until the lessons are learnt. To the contrary, people who are not conscious enough choose to ignore the pain. They choose to stay in their comfort zone, thus often losing the opportunity to learn and grow.

Growth is associated with making changes. Many people are not willing to change, because making a change might be overwhelming and uncomfortable. It might involve risks, and there might be more time, energy and money required for the change. However, without changes, there comes stagnation, which is even worse than the pain caused by growth. Look at who you are today, you are never the same as yesterday, and will never be the same as tomorrow. Through growth, we evolve.

Let us face growth with full awareness, acceptance and openness. Embrace the pain and sufferings associated with these experiences, be aware of the learning curve, don't have unreasonably high expectations, and eventually you will live a fulfilling life

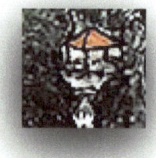

## Suggestions

Keep an open heart to all kinds of life lessons, including newly gained knowledge from all new experiences.

## Inner Search

Am I accepting my growing process?
Am I capable of handling the pain that growth brings into my life?
Where and how do I feel that I grow the most?

## Affirmation

**From all the hardship and discomfort in my life, I grow tremendously.**

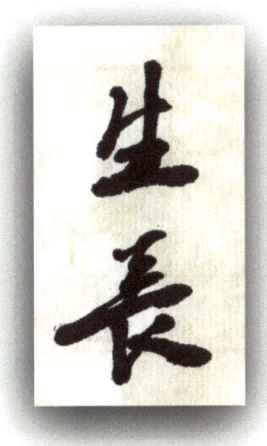

# *Maturity*

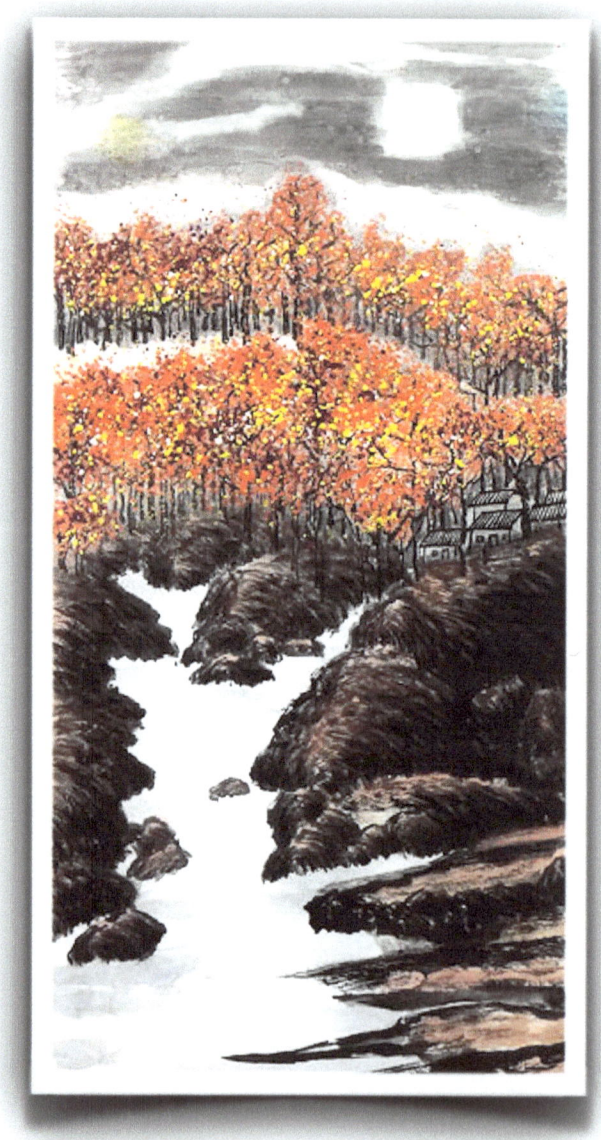

Find Your Inner Truth ~ YINUO TIAN ~ 30

*"Part of spiritual and emotional maturity is recognizing that it's not like you're going to try to fix yourself and become a different person. You remain the same person, but you become awakened."*

*~Jack Kornfield~*

Autumn is the season of harvest and maturity. After experiencing all kinds of turbulences, seeing through the storms and rainbows in life, this is the season when we can evaluate what lessons have been learnt and how much we have grown from all the hard work; whether or not we fall into the category of "maturity" and can reap whatever we have sown.

I remember that when I was little, my parents' friends and our family relatives always commented that I was a "mature and independent" kid. Deep in my heart, I liked this comment a lot, because I saw it as a compliment saying that I am a kid with good manners. Since my youth, I look up to people who are mature.

As a grown up, now I understand maturity better and I still admire people who demonstrate maturity in different aspects of their lives. First and foremost is emotional maturity. Emotionally matured people are aware of their emotions, they made decisions based on principles, and not emotions. These people are emotionally stable, thus they can manage situations well even when everything around them seems out of control. Being emotionally mature, means we are not simply reacting to what is happening, but are able to be proactive to live the life by our values. People get along with an emotionally stable person, whose flattery and criticism is more objective, they are responsible for their actions and can thus be trusted.

Next aspect is mental maturity. Mentally mature people can communicate with efficiency, and know exactly how to express themselves. Mental maturity also makes one a good listener, able to analyze the situation with mental clarity, process information correctly and give constructive advise accordingly. People feel comfortable sharing their stories with a mentally mature person, because they feel heard, understood, without being judged.

In addition, maturity is also very important in the financial area. Financial maturity is the discipline in spending, saving and investing. It is the ability to manage the income and expenditure at ease, to allocate resources in a wise way. Knowing exactly when to spend, how to spend, work within a financial budget, is a good way to learning financial maturity.

Last but not least, is spiritual maturity. It is the awareness of the spiritual relationship with the Divine. As we grow, we never stop seeking wisdom. With spiritual maturity, we become more grateful, open our heart to accept, ground ourselves in humility and recognize our authenticity in the divine. Thus, we become our true selves.

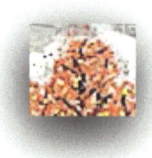

### *Suggestions*

Be present and mindful. Observe your life experiences as if you are watching a movie. See everything from a more objective perspective and develop maturity slowly in this way.

### *Inner Search*

Am I capable of seeing my future in a mature way?
Am I mature in my actions, thoughts and choices?
How could I handle my challenging situation with more maturity?

### *Affirmation*

**I am developing maturity in all aspects,
and am enjoying the happiness and fulfillment that it
brings into my life.**

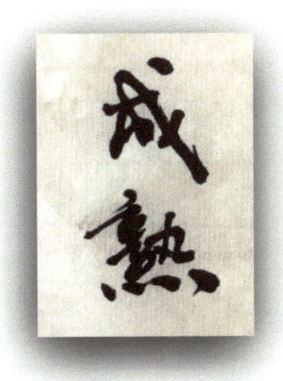

# *Wisdom*

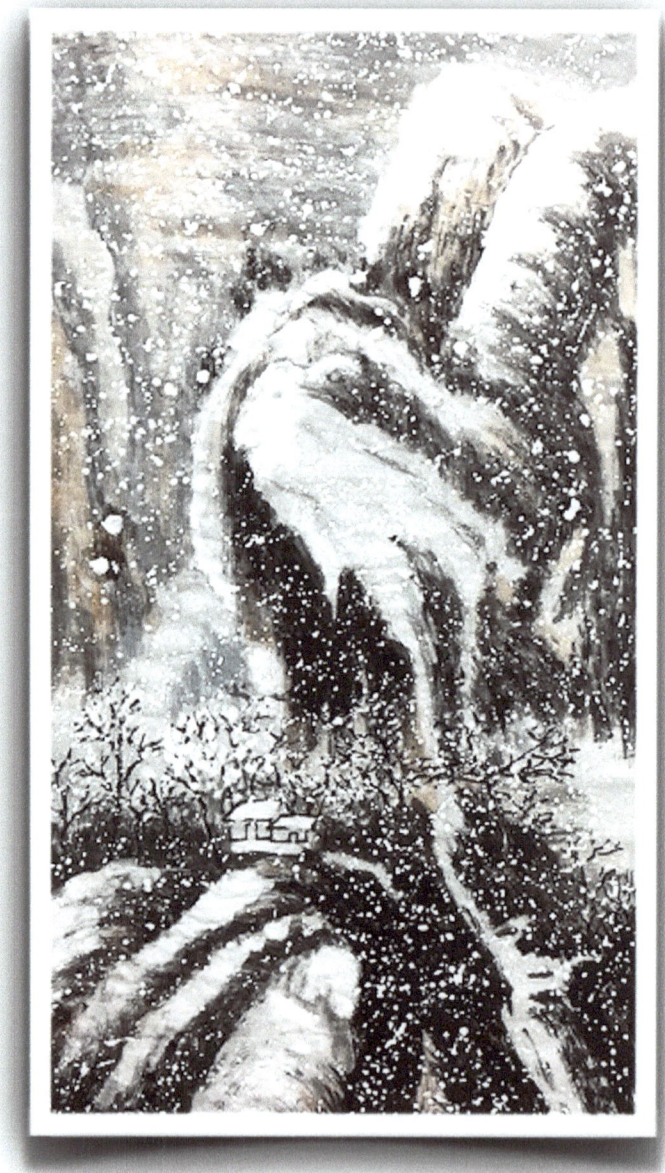

Find Your Inner Truth ~ YINUO TIAN ~ 34

*"Wisdom is not a product of schooling but of the lifelong attempt to acquire it."*

*~Albert Einstein~*

Wisdom used to be one of the widely pursued virtues in almost all cultures. In modern society, it is greatly undervalued. Individual and social wisdom is no longer appreciated as much as before, due to the change in social values. However, there are still people like you and me, who wish to pursue wisdom in our daily life, because we understand its value in helping us live a happier life.

People have many misunderstandings about wisdom. Some think wisdom is equivalent to knowledge. Some think wisdom is the same as being smart. Some think we naturally become wise when we grow older. Unfortunately, none of the above is true. What is wisdom? It is hard to give it a simple definition, but we can understand wisdom as a blend of many positive traits, which enable us to make the right decision at the right time.

Wisdom is not something that can be acquired overnight. Living a life filled with wisdom takes intention, focus and commitment. It requires great determination and a lot of effort to cultivate. How can we cultivate wisdom?

One important way is to slow down and pause. We are living in a fast-paced society. Everything is rushed. Often times we are forced to do things under pressure, and we make mistakes or get into trouble due to lack of consideration. Wise people are effective, but they do not rush to get things done. They take time to discern, analyze, and consider all the consequences of their actions.

Learning to spend time in silence is another way to cultivate wisdom. Of course we all have such moments when we get a glimpse of wisdom while speaking to someone or listening to their experiences. But do not forget the term "inner wisdom". When we are in total silence, we get in touch with our inner wisdom, which is always there to give us direction and insight.

Reading and journaling also help you develop wisdom. Through reading widely, we continue learning, about different people, culture, history, and various subjects. Through journaling, we reflect on the knowledge and experiences we have already gained, and we get to know how to do actions accordingly. Sometimes it is also helpful to ask ourselves - what would a wise person do if they were in my situation. The answer will guide you to make a wiser decision.

In addition, to be wise, we need to have more empathy, compassion and love. Put yourself into other people's shoes. A wise person is always able to grasp the whole situation, while taking another's thoughts and feelings into consideration. A wise man is always radiating loving energy and is therefore respected by many.

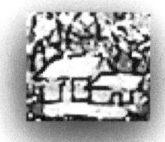

### *Suggestions*

Start meditating and be committed to it on a daily basis.
It is a great way to gain wisdom in all aspects of your life.

### *Inner Search*

Am I wise?
Can I tap into my source of wisdom?
How could I act wiser each and every day?

### *Affirmation*

**I am committed to cultivate wisdom in my daily life.
I am wiser every day.**

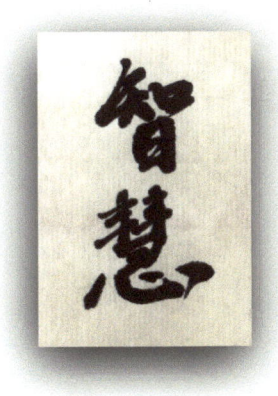

# Self~reflection

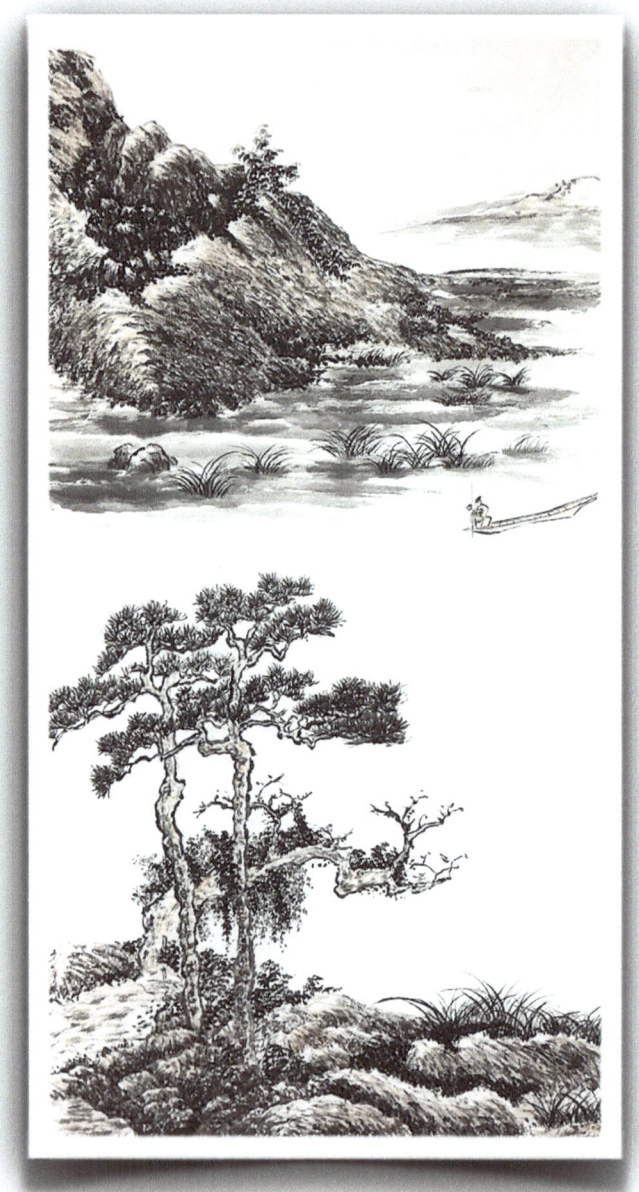

Find Your Inner Truth ~ YINUO TIAN ~ 38

*"The greatest of faults, is to be conscious of none."*

*~ Thomas Carlyle ~*

"How time flies!" Nowadays we like to comment on how fast time goes by. It feels like we are forever running on a treadmill, but many times we get into the momentum of running so much that we forget where we are heading to, and when we are supposed to stop. We do bump our head here and there, or go off the track every now and then. Eventually, we may find ourselves either repeating the same things again and again, without getting desired results, or we are totally lost about what we are doing.

Self-reflection is a human ability to introspect own thoughts, behaviors, patterns, and tendencies. It helps us realign with our goals and purpose, find the answers to all questions we have in mind, become a better human being, in order to live a more successful and fulfilled life. Some of us think it is insignificant to self reflect; some of us keep moving forward, saying there is no time for self reflection. Until one day, we find ourselves not able to keep up. Then we stop, take a step back, re-evaluate what has happened and start to be aware about the messages that are coming into our lives. Something has shifted, now we are able to see the bigger picture and re-organize our daily activities more effectively.

Many of us are familiar with the saying, that the outer world is a reflection of the inner world. Knowingly or unknowingly, we are creating our own experiences and shaping our surroundings through our thoughts. Are you seeing struggles, fear, anger and chaos in your life? Or are you experiencing love, harmony, peace and calming energy? With self reflection, we can consciously re-program our thoughts, and in turn create our own desired realities. Begin self observing today. Be more conscious of which type of people show up, and what incidences are happening in your daily life. Is this what you really want to experience?

Another wonderful way to practice self reflection is through journaling. By cultivating the habit of journaling, you can bring out many positive transformations. As we all know, our monkey mind is always busy, so that we can seldom catch up with all the ideas in our mind. However, if we journal, we are able to handle the ideas tangibly. There is a high chance that we become an actual goal achiever, instead of just a day dreamer. It is specially important to journal on occasions such as new year, birthdays, or major events. It is also a great habit to set aside a regular time for journaling that can be monthly, weekly or even daily.

Really make effort to self reflect. Through practice, we can all live our dreams and become a better version of ourselves.

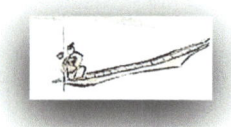

### *Suggestions*

Keep a journal, set a specific time for daily journaling.
Make sure you are not disturbed during that time and do not rush through the writing.
Write as if you are talking to your best friend.

### *Inner Search*

Am I reflecting on myself regularly?
What self reflection skills do I wish to develop?
How can I improve the quality of my life through self reflection?

### *Affirmation*

**I am completely aware of my surroundings
and I am totally responsible for the life I create.**

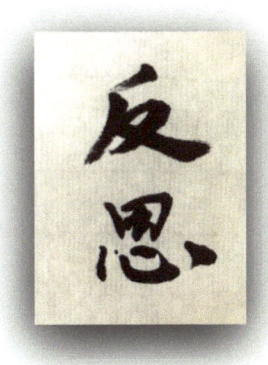

# *Blessings in disguise*

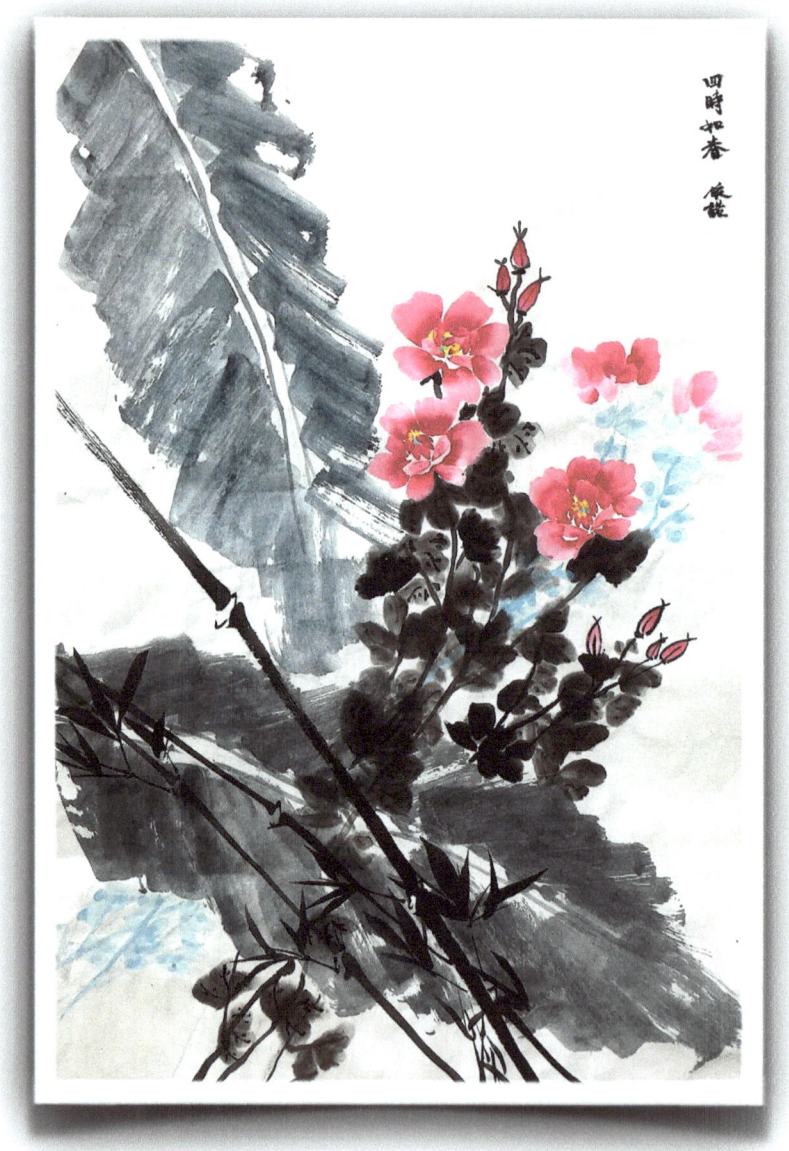

Find Your Inner Truth ~ YINUO TIAN ~ *42*

*"There is blessing hidden in every trial in life, but you have to be willing to open your heart to see them."*

*~ Anonymous ~*

Many people have such experiences in life - the seemingly bad encounters bring precious life gifts soon after. We call them blessings in disguise. Of course, not many of us can see these blessings right away, especially when we are deeply preoccupied with the short-term problems which we are facing.

What is your reaction when something undesirable happens? Do you get emotional? Do you complain? Do you get angry? Do you fight against it? These are all normal reactions when we are not accepting what is happening to us. We try to play the role of the big brother and have everything under our control. When things go out of control, we go into the state of denial, which leads us to many other negative emotions. As Mark Twain once said, "Denial (Da Nile) ain't just a river in Egypt". When denial continues, we experience similar patterns again and again, until we finally learn the lesson. This could take a few days, weeks, months, years, or even a life time.

How can you break out of the patterns? Is there a way out?
Actually there is. Denial can also lead us to acceptance. What is required is just a change in perspective. Instead of looking at the short-term losses, we can choose to take ourselves out of the picture and look at it from the distance.

To begin, acknowledge and accept whatever challenges and setbacks you are facing. Next, have faith that all the hardships in life are teaching you something very valuable. Truly believe the results will turn out to be inspiring and beneficial, to yourselves, as well as to others.

Easier said than done. The change in perspective may require lots of practice for some of us. Especially when we are having a difficult time, we tend to lose the ability to think straight. Whenever this happens, re-evaluate the past challenges and problems in your life. Do you see the outcome they brought about? Do you agree with the saying "everything happens for your highest good"? How would things differ if you could fully control and run your own scenes?

I used the approach of seeing things from a far distance for many of my past experiences, and I could not be more grateful for what happened and how they lead me to my current path. Through this practice, I learnt to see the beauty in everything. Now I am a strong believer of blessings in disguise. I truly hope you too can practice this in your life, so that something wonderful comes out of it each time you meet a challenge.

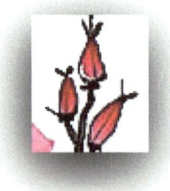

## *Suggestions*

Make notes that remind you of the message "Everything happens for my highest good".
You may paste it on places that you see frequently, or keep it in your wallet or journal.
When you are experiencing life's challenges, repeat the messages of these notes,
or meditate on them.

## *Inner Search*

Am I able to recognize the blessings in disguise?
What are the biggest blessings in disguise in my life?
How can I find more blessings in my life?

## *Affirmation*

**I open my heart to see the beauty in everything
and every encounter in my life.**

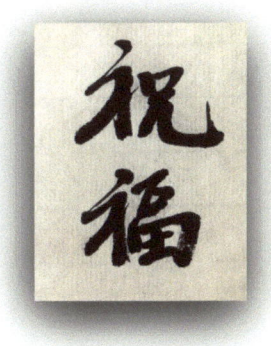

# *Overcoming obstacles*

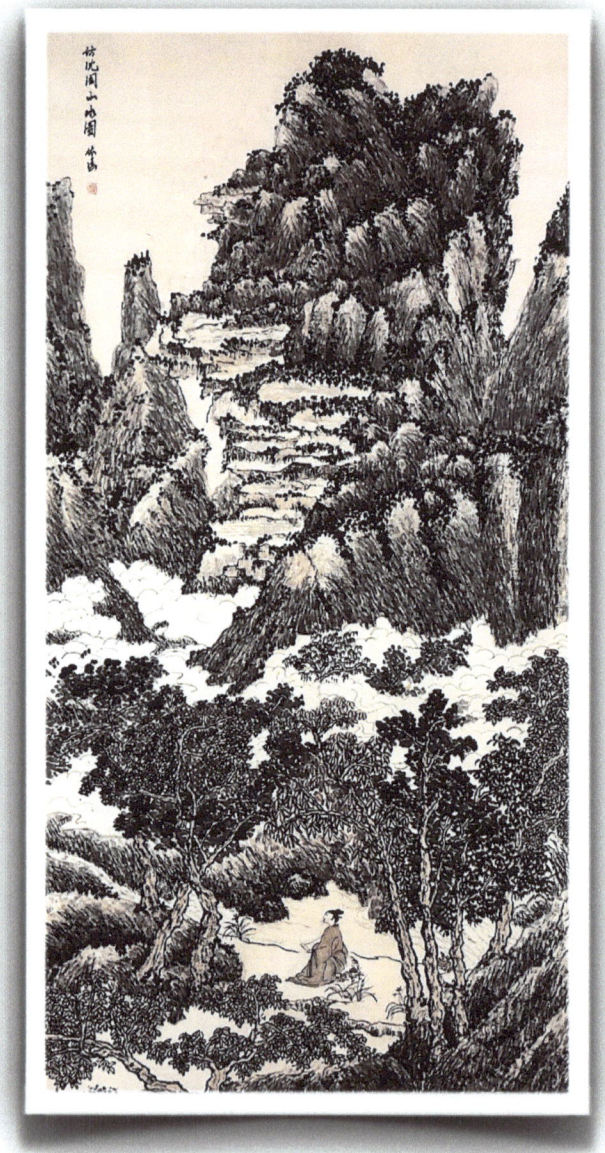

Find Your Inner Truth ~ YINUO TIAN ~ 46

*"Smooth seas do not make skillful sailors."*

*~African Proverb ~*

People all around the world face challenges and obstacles in life, big or small, we all face them everyday.

Sometimes the obstacles can give us such significant distress that we cannot cope with it. When we are feeling pressure, we want to quit. When we have a new project in hand, for sure there will be new challenges and sometimes obstacles that we cannot anticipate at all. In such circumstances, it is a conscious choice to quit or continue. Imagine the majority of people quitting whenever they come across an obstacle. Our world would be completely different from what it is now. We would definitely not be able to enjoy abundant development in economics, technologies, and culture. Overcoming the obstacles is a way to grow and transform.

Handling obstacles requires clarity. First and for most, we need to reinforce the goal we have chosen. There must be total clarity about what the goal is, and what we are going to accomplish. Once the goal is set, stay committed to it. At the same time, be aware of any obstacles that come your way.

Overcoming obstacles also requires a strong and focused mind. Nothing can shake the determination of a goal achiever. If you feel fear and other negative emotions in the subconscious mind, acknowledge them and move forward. Sometimes the obstacle can be too big to handle, in such cases, break it into smaller ones or categorize it so that help can be obtained from professionals.

The path towards reaching the goal can be a lonely and boring one, however, we need to stay focused. Avoid distractions with other projects, no matter if they are related to your current one or not. The concept of "multi-tasking" does not really work well. With limited attention and energy span, we can only do well one thing at a time. Only after the current goal is achieved, you can set a new goal and work on it wholeheartedly.

It always feels nice when a goal is accomplished. Quitters will never have a chance to experience this. Never let negative emotions ruin what is coming your way. Be brave and take initiatives, keep your thoughts on the final positive outcome, manifest the life that you dream about.

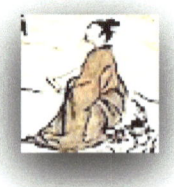

### *Suggestions*

Develop your determination and focus by setting periodic goals.
Record the whole process.
Remember, one goal at a time.

### *Inner Search*

Am I capable of overcoming obstacles?
What was my biggest obstacle in life?
What would help me overcome obstacles easier?

### *Affirmation*

**I face obstacles bravely and overcome them easily.**

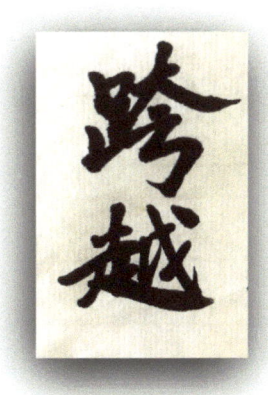

# *Letting go*

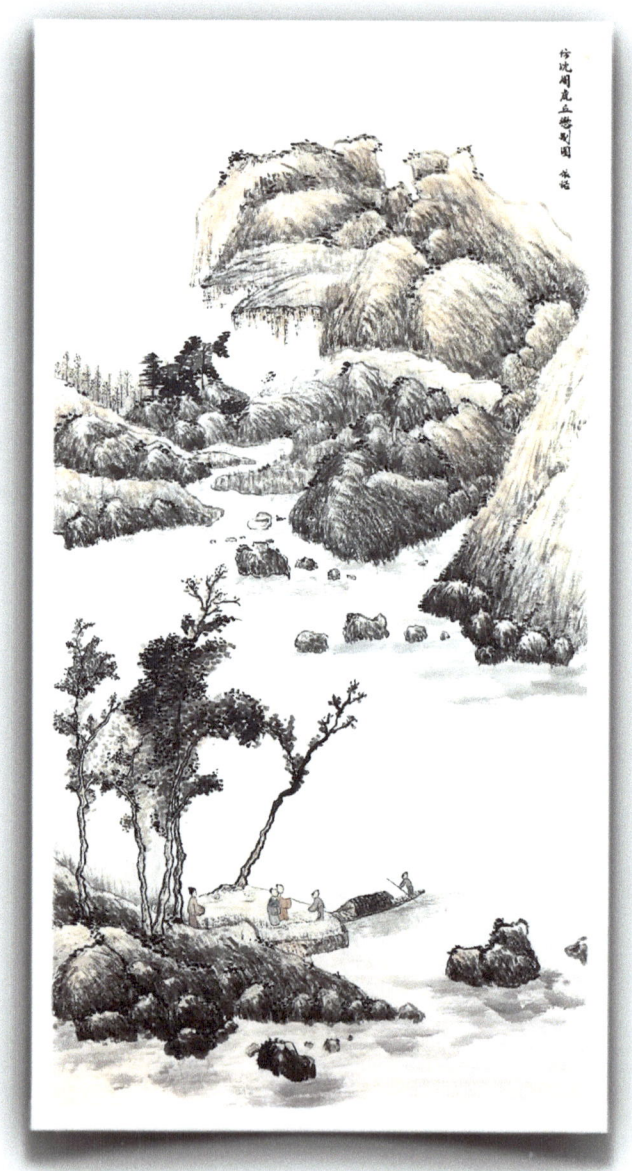

Find Your Inner Truth ~ YINUO TIAN ~ 50

*"Some of us think holding on makes us strong. But sometimes it is letting go."*

*~Herman Hesse~*

Many of us have had the experience of falling into water. The first reaction for majority of people is the struggle to come up for air. But our muscles harden when we get nervous; instead of going up, we tend to sink even deeper. If we are able to let go of the fear and anxieties in the mind, muscles will become relaxed, and we will easily float to the water surface.

We all know that clinging onto something or someone is not a comfortable feeling. We tense up, both physically and emotionally. But still, be it a living being, material possession, expectation, we tend to hold on to it. We like to have control. It feels good when we are "on top of everything". However, we have to admit that things can get out of control every now and then. We will suffer during such an occasion if we do not know how to let go. Sometimes we are too emotionally attached to someone or something, we feel insecure and incomplete if we let go. However, the more we cling onto it, the further it slips away from us.

Letting go is something that we need to experience, because only then we begin to appreciate it. We might feel insecure, anxious, or powerless at the beginning, but after this brave decision has been made, we experience wonderful gifts from the universe. Trust the universe completely, we understand everything happens for a reason, and the divine timing always turns out to be better than a plan we make in our little human mind. In my personal experience, whenever I chose to trust and let go, new opportunities, wonderful people and experiences came into my life.

Letting go is not as easy as it sounds. I practice letting go in two stages. First, I let go of something that no longer serves me. For example, I check through my wardrobe every two or three months, to see whether there are clothes or accessories that I no longer want to keep. If so, I pack them up, donate or give away. Same procedure applies to other household categories.

The second stage of practice requires more self-awareness and discipline, as I work with the attachments that I have. Whenever I notice that I am attached to something, a person, or life experience, I reflect on a series of questions: why am I attached to it? What do I want to get out of it? What happens if I let go? Can I handle the worst-case scenario if I let go? After self-reflecting on these questions, I usually feel very relieved. Because I realize the worst-case scenario is not that bad, and I can handle it very well when I treat it as a life lesson to be learnt.

When God closes one door, he always opens another. Just remember that if you have to let go of something, there is something better waiting to come into your life. Be brave, be adventurous. Accept life as it happens.

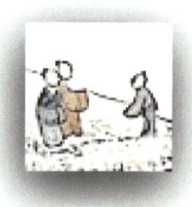

### *Suggestions*

Start by re-evaluating your material belongings and letting go
of those that no longer serve you.
During this process, your perspective will slowly change.
You will naturally begin to let go on an emotional, mental and spiritual level.

### *Inner Search*

Am I capable of letting go?
What is the attachment that I need to let go of at this moment?
How will I feel if and when I let go of this?

### *Affirmation*

**I trust that everything happening in my life is for my highest good.
I am willing to let go, and just flow.**

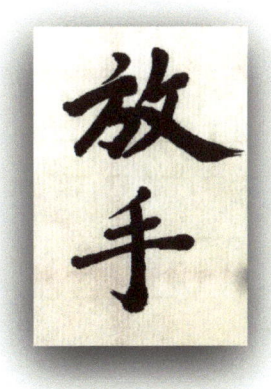

# *Prosperity*

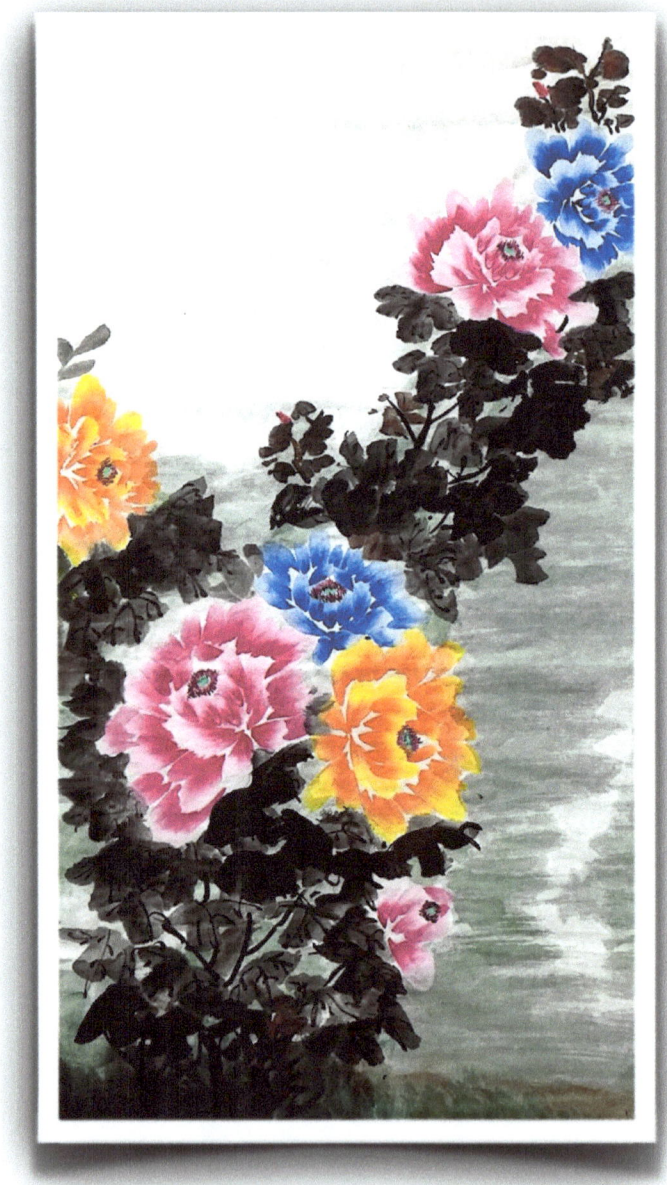

Find Your Inner Truth ~ YINUO TIAN ~ *54*

*"When I chased after money, I never had enough.
When I got my life on purpose & focused on giving of myself
and everything that arrived into my life, then I was prosperous."*

*~ Wayne Dyer ~*

When we talk about prosperity, we often relate to it through money, social status, and power. In this modern world, money is no longer just a medium of exchange for goods and services, but has gradually become a more powerful tool. It seems, that with money we can buy anything we want, connect to any sort of power, or even solve physical, emotional or mental problems, temporarily or for good.

People of all ages are chasing after money. Yes, all of us have bills to pay, we need money to maintain our comfortable lifestyle. However, once we achieve a certain lifestyle, we can ask ourselves and honestly answer, do we ever feel that we have enough? What is the burning desire behind the scenes which keeps us chasing after more money? What are we addicted to?

Everyone has a different intention when it comes to living a prosperous life. Some people want to make loads of money to build their own empire and leave behind a good reputation; some people want to be more socially influential through financial success, so that they can help and serve people in need.

No matter what the initial intention is, it is important to prevent the occurrence of greed. In fact, many people forget what they were initially seeking while playing the money chasing game, because they were seduced by greed. Any beginning good intention can burn into ashes by greedy addiction to money, power and social status.

Prosperity is also related to good fortune. It's a popular word in blessings. We wish each other a prosperous life on birthdays, for new business ventures, and before the beginning of new year. When I hear these words, I always feel the fullness in my heart. It is never about lacking. Isn't that interesting? When we chase after prosperity, we project the lack of it, not having enough of it, but actually it is quite the opposite. Prosperity is about growing and flourishing; it is everyone's birth right to enjoy.

In order to live a prosperous life, we need to connect to our life purpose, set clear intentions and have positive, affirmative thoughts. How can we accomplish that? Continuously nurture the heart and watch your thoughts and behavior. Be present and live with mindfulness. Once we are clear about our life path, it is not difficult to feel that we are provided with everything we need, we always have enough to accomplish our goals. Only then, our life becomes prosperous.

### *Suggestions*

Keep track of the small incidences which make you feel prosperous.
You may want to keep a separate diary for this purpose.
Always remember to keep a thankful heart and give back to the society.

### *Inner Search*

Do I recognize prosperity in my life?
What effort am I making to increase and cultivate my prosperity?
Do I handle situations with an open and prosperous mindset?

### *Affirmation*

**I am crystal clear about my life purpose.
Prosperity comes into my life easily and continuously.**

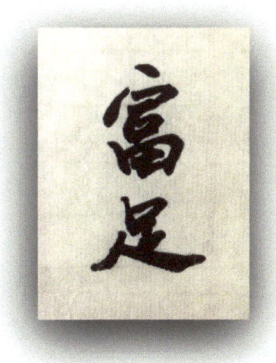

# *Happiness*

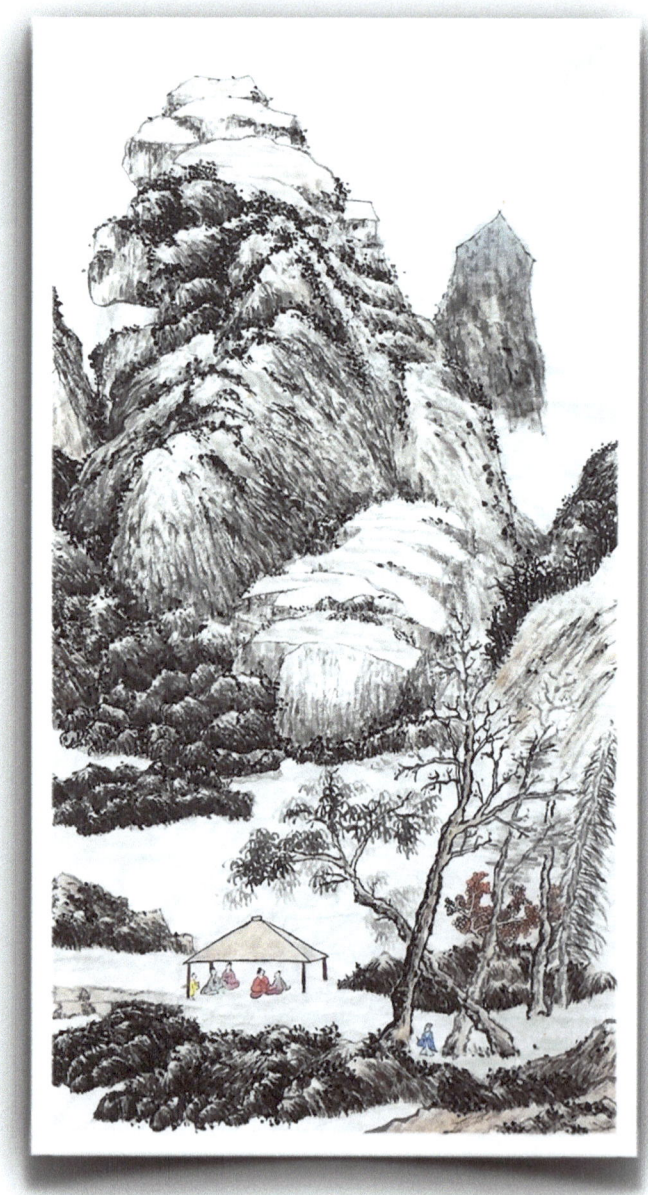

Find Your Inner Truth ~ YINUO TIAN ~ *58*

*"Don't let your happiness depend on something you may lose."*

*~C. S. Lewis~*

We all pursue happiness in life. Happiness is our birthright.

There are many different paths that lead to happiness. Some of us find happiness in getting material possessions, some in reading books, traveling, or doing creative projects. There is nothing wrong with the pursuit of happiness. We can do whatever makes us happy and vibrant, as long as it does not violate the law or rights of other people.

When you feel happy, many physiological changes occur in your body. For example, there is a chemical change in your brain, which gives you a feeling of pleasure, a rush of passion and joy. This helps fight stress and pain, boosts your immune system, and supports longevity.

In addition, doing a project which brings you happiness, stimulates the power of creativity. We usually get more creative ideas when we are doing something we really like. Imagine you are sitting with co-workers at a meeting. If the meeting is about something that you are not really interested in, the discussion becomes very routine and boring. To the contrary, if you are very passionate about the project, you will come up with tons of additional creative ideas to put into implementation. I am sure you can easily visualize these two kinds of meetings in your mind, including how they make you feel your facial expressions and behavior. Which meeting do you wish to participate in?

From a spiritual perspective, when we are pursuing happiness, we are getting in touch with our true self. Therefore, the process of pursuing happiness is a process of learning about yourself. Initially we probably believe that by obtaining something or doing something we will live a happy and joyful life; but maybe after some time we find out such happiness does not last. Many of us pursued such external journey, but eventually we will find the fountain of happiness rooted within us. True happiness, the purpose and meaning of our existence are always within us, waiting to be revealed. It does not depend on anything else, but is always accessible to us at any time, and any place.

As I mentioned earlier, we all have different ways of pursuing of happiness. One man's trash is another man's treasure. To me, I connect with the happiness frequency by doing projects that I am passionate about, and through meditation. Meditation is one of the most important practices in my daily morning routine. It does not need to be very long, a simple ten-minute morning meditation is long enough to set a positive tone for the rest of the day, and brings about positive vibrations for myself, people I encounter, and my living environment.

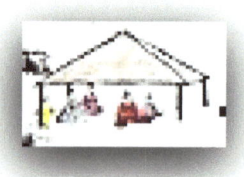

### *Suggestions*

Do something that makes you happy. It can be your hobby, a short personal time, or any project that you feel passionate about.

### *Inner Search*

What is happiness for me?
Am I happy at this moment?
What would make me the happiest in my life?

### *Affirmation*

**Happiness comes into my life easily.
I am living a happy and meaningful life.**

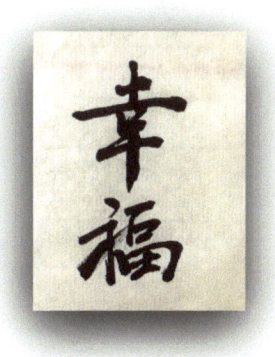

# *Abundance*

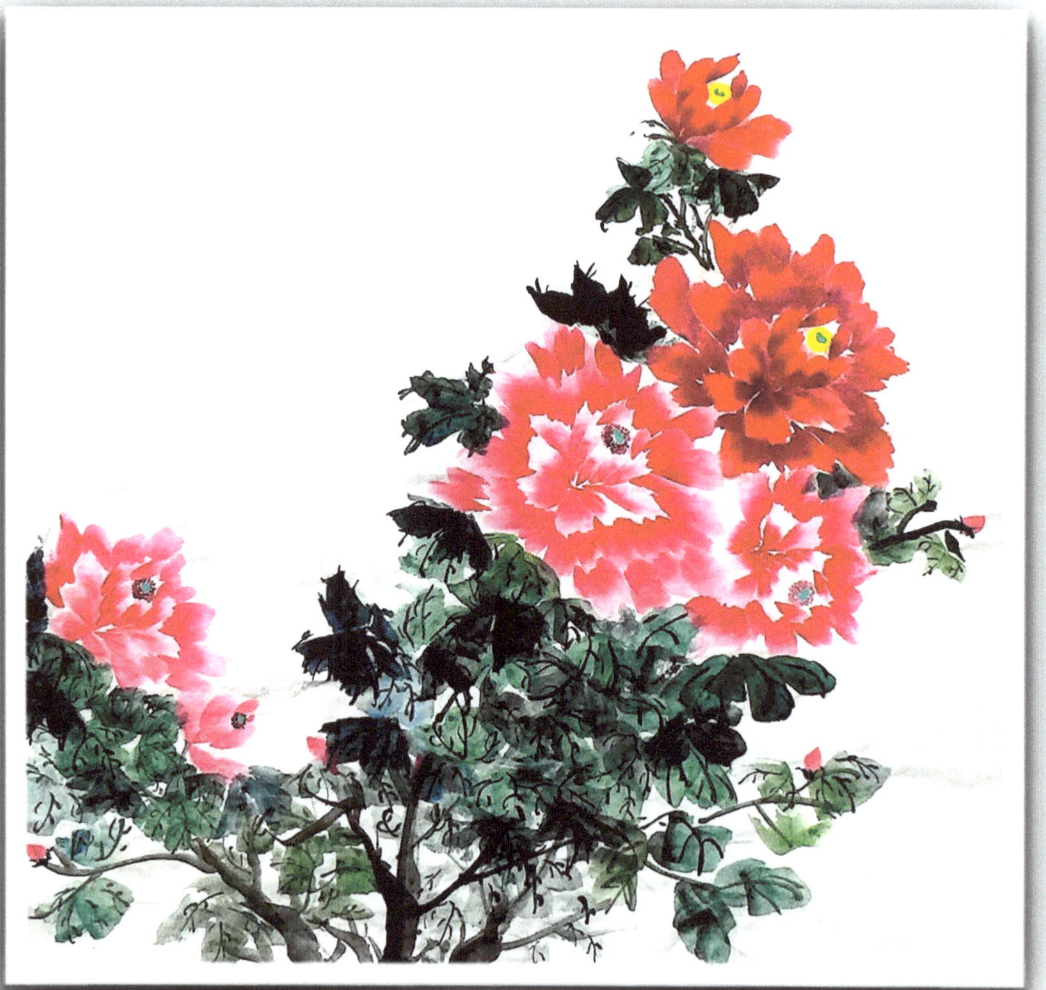

Find Your Inner Truth ~ YINUO TIAN ~ *62*

*"Abundance is not something we acquire. It is something we tune into."*

*~Wayne Dyer~*

Abundance is related to the words enough, satisfaction, plenty, and riches. It is not just about money and material possessions, but also health, love, relationships, career, and general views about life. The opposite of abundance is deficiency and inadequacy, which are usually caused by fear and worry.

There is an old story about an elderly man who owned a small business in a tiny town, selling pancakes on the street. His pancakes were so delicious that he slowly gained recognition from many customers, his business expanded and he was able to recruit more people and open a chain of shops in the same town. He was doing very well and quickly gained lots of money and fame. One day, the old man's son who just graduated from college came back home from a big city, and told his father about a recession that was going to happen. The son explained to his father what recession is, and also suggested to him how he could lower the cost by reducing the quality of his products. The old man followed his son's advice, but the customers were not happy, the sales went down and he had to close down a few of his branches. Following these events, cash flow was affected, so the old man further reduced the quality of his products, which created further dissatisfactions from customers, so eventually he had to close down more shops. After this occurred, the old man was very proud of his son's predictions and suggestions, and thought his son was totally right about the recession. The old man's experiences show us clearly how an inadequate mindset, fear and worries can manifest a totally different life. The old man just simply believed his son, instead of trusting his own original inner vision.

Abundance is a state of mind. There are people who are resourceful, live a comfortable life, however are always afraid that their resources will be taken or stolen by others. That is not an abundant mindset, which will eventually affect their life in a negative way, just as is happened to the old man.

If we look at this concept at a deeper level, it is not hard to understand that behind this inadequate mindset, lies the common belief that we need to compete with others in order to get what we desire. Many people tend to hide their resources or opportunities from "competitors" in order to succeed. It is important to know that there is enough of everything to go around. The universe is providing everything to us, we all have access to unlimited resources. We do not get deprived when somebody else gains. All we need to do is align our frequency with the universe. Once this alignment is achieved, we can truly enjoy our birthright to live a joyful, fulfilled, abundant and meaningful life.

How can you cultivate a mindset of abundance? When you see a glass of water, do you perceive it as half filled, or half empty? In other words, are you focusing your energy on gratitude about the water, or anxiety on the emptiness and not having enough water? Gratitude is the essential factor in manifesting anything in your life. With gratitude, the sense of satisfaction, and fulfillment, is naturally generated.

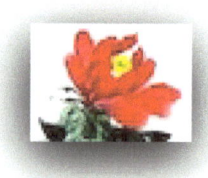

### *Suggestions*

Keep a separate "gratitude journal". Every morning upon awakening, write a few lines about what you are grateful for. You may also keep the journal with you wherever you go, and write down all the grateful moments during the day.

### *Inner Search*

What does abundance mean to me at this moment?
Am I feeling abundant?
What prevents me from feeling abundant?

### *Affirmation*

**I am grateful that I am living an abundant life.**

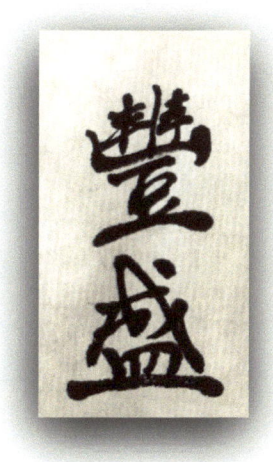

# *Journey of the Soul*

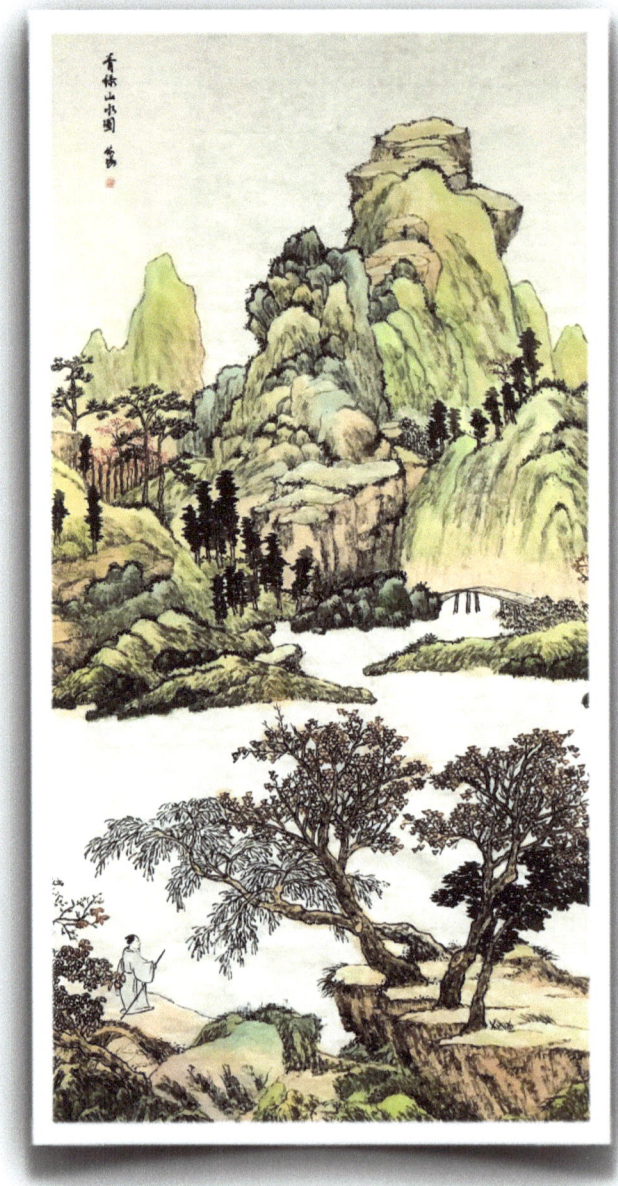

Find Your Inner Truth ~ YINUO TIAN ~ *66*

*"The human soul is on its journey from the law to love,*
*from discipline to liberation,*
*from the moral plane to the spiritual."*

*~Rabindranath Tagore~*

Who am I? Where did I come from? Where will I go after death? Many of us have asked these questions at certain stages in life.

Our body is our temple. We were born into this temple; however, we are not limited to this temple. When major life experiences reveal themselves one by one, we start to realize that we are soul beings, and we have lessons to learn, a purpose to fulfill. There is no doubt that we live in our temple and need do our earthly duties. For example, we perform our roles in our family and social circles, we make ends meet, pay bills, go through education, collaborate with others at work. During this period, we make conscious or unconscious choices, and go through certain hurdles in life. Through the ups and downs, we begin to understand ourselves and our surroundings, gain some wisdom, and slowly we manage to have a glimpse of the true self and our higher purpose in life.

Those hurdles and challenges we experienced are the lessons meant to be learned. You may have observed that you tend to meet similar types of people all the time, or have to handle many similar circumstances. These reveal the lesson to be learned. And the lesson is going to repeat itself in different life scenarios until you learn. Once the lesson is mastered, you progress to the next one. And this way, the journey goes on and on, through this entire lifetime, and beyond.

Whether you consider yourself spiritual or not, it is important for you to at least cultivate a few simple practices, which can help you re-connect to your true self. One of the practices I do daily is a combination of breath work and meditation. It brings me inner peace and calmness throughout, I get more clarity each time, and after the practice I am able to make conscious decisions.

This is very important when realizing your soul's purpose and journey. Be consciously aware to your thoughts, intentions, and behavior. All these help reveal lessons in your life bit by bit.

As a soul being, understanding yourself and the journey of your soul will bring you fulfillment, satisfaction and purpose. Through the deeper understanding, you will also cultivate love, trust towards others, empowerment and will be able to live your life to the fullest.

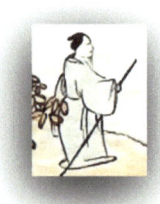

### *Suggestions*

Maintain the spiritual practice that you are comfortable with,
constantly be aware of your inner voice, and connect to your inner self.
The guidance is always there if you are willing to listen.

### *Inner Search*

Do I recognize the journey of my soul?
What is my life purpose?
What would fulfill me and my life purpose?

### *Affirmation*

**I am clear about my path and life purpose.
I am fulfilling my life's destiny.**

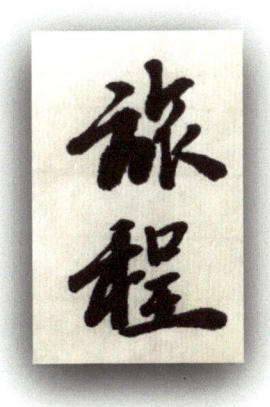

Find Your Inner Truth ~ YINUO TIAN ~ *70*

# Acknowledgments

First of all, I would like to express my sincere gratitude to my mentor Dr. Sabrina Mesko, without whom this book would not have been possible. Sabrina has been continuously inspiring and supporting me since we met, years ago. She witnessed my spiritual growth throughout the years.

I am also grateful to my respected Chinese painting teacher, Ms. Wang Shilan, for teaching me to paint with great patience and encouragements. All the paintings in this book were completed under Ms. Wang's valuable guidance.

I would also like to express my deep appreciation to all my teachers, guides, and friends, who have been such a positive influence in my life and helped open many wonderful, spiritual gates.

Lastly, I would like to extend my gratitude to my dearest parents, who are always there for me, with lots of love and moral support.

Find Your Inner Truth ~ YINUO TIAN ~ 72

# *About the Author*

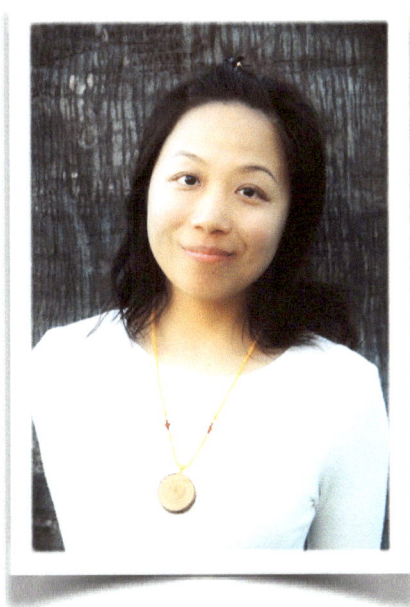

Originally from China, Yinuo received full scholarship from the Singapore government in 1999 and has been studying and working in Singapore ever since. She holds a degree in Electrical and Computer Engineering, and a Master's in Applied Finance.

In 2002, the health benefits of yoga drew Yinuo into various yoga practices. Soon she began teaching yoga and gradually explored different styles, including Hatha, Ashtanga, Sivananda, Yin Yoga, Kundalini Yoga, Yoga Therapy and Iyengar Yoga. Yinuo was also personally initiated into Kriya Yoga by Guruji Shibendu Lahiri, the great grandson of the great Master Lahiri Mahasaya, and has been a dedicated practitioner ever since then.

Yinuo is a Yoga Alliance Experienced Registered Yoga Teacher (E-RYT500) and a certified Pilates Instructor. She graduated from SVYASA (India) and holds Post Graduate Diploma in Yoga Therapy.

With her great passion and love for therapy and healing, Yinuo dived into studying various healing modalities throughout the following years. She is a Master Teacher in Usui Reiki and Kundalini Reiki, Master in Komyo Reiki, Certified Mudra Teacher and Therapist, practitioner of various healing techniques including Emotional Freedom Techniques (EFT, aka Tapping), Magnified Healing, Oneness Deeksha healing, Sound Therapy with Tibetan Singing Bowls and Tuning Forks, Psych-K, Shamanic healing, and Star Magic healing. She studied numerology, astrology, Tarot card, Lenormand card, which she uses in her work. In addition, Yinuo is a USA certified Clinical Aromatherapist graduated from National Aromatherapy Holistic Association (NAHA), USA.

Yinuo teaches and guides her students based on their specific needs and goals. She helps them work through challenges, when working in stressful environments and delights in nurturing new yoga teachers by conducting various Yoga Teacher Training Courses. Yinuo enjoys sharing her findings and experiences with all her students and readers, and loves to inspire them to realize their full potential. She incorporates all different healing modalities into her work and has created a very unique transformative method. To Yinuo, Yoga is a life long practice.

Visit the Author online at **yogabijaa.com**

www.ingramcontent.com/pod-product-compliance
Lightning Source LLC
Chambersburg PA
CBHW051201220526
45473CB00003B/856